How Do Airplanes FLY?

Zachary Williams

The Rosen Publishing Group's

READING ROOM
Collection™

New York

Published in 2002 by The Rosen Publishing Group, Inc.
29 East 21st Street, New York, NY 10010

Copyright © 2002 by The Rosen Publishing Group,

First Library Edition 2002

Book Design: Haley Wilson

Photo Credits: Cover, pp. 10, 19 © Michael Agliolo/International Stock; pp. 4, 7 © Bettman/Corbis; p. 8 © Joe McDonald/Corbis; p. 9 © Stockbyte; p. 12 © Bob Jacobson/International Stock; p. 15 by Ryan Giuliani; p. 16 © Scott Barrow/International Stock; p. 21 © George Ancona/ International Stock.

Williams, Zachary, 1972-
    How do airplanes fly? / Zachary Williams.
        p. cm. — (Rosen Publishing Group's reading room collection)
    Summary: Explains briefly why airplanes are able to fly and notes
certain historical milestones in the field of aeronautics.
    ISBN 0-8239-3723-2 (library binding)
    1. Aeronautics--Juvenile literature. 2. Airplanes—Juvenile
literature. [1. Aeronautics. 2. Airplanes.] I. Title. II. Series.
    TL547 .W643 2002
    629.13—dc21
                                        2001007035

Manufactured in the United States of America

For More Information
Phoenix Sky Harbor International Airport: Kids Section
http:www.phxaviation.com/skyharbr/kids/

Contents

The Science of Flying

People have always wanted to fly. Many years ago, some people tried to copy birds by building huge wings. The wings didn't help them fly. People didn't understand the science of flying.

In the early 1900s, Orville and Wilbur Wright did **experiments** to learn the secret of flying. They built and tested the first gas-powered airplane, the *Wright Flyer 1*.

Orville and Wilbur Wright became the first people to learn how to fly successfully.

The First Flight

On December 17, 1903, the Wright brothers made the first gas-powered flight near Kitty Hawk, North Carolina. With Orville at the controls, the *Wright Flyer 1* stayed in the air for twelve seconds and flew 121 feet. Wilbur flew the *Wright Flyer 1* a total of 852 feet. The flight lasted fifty-nine seconds!

After many years of experimenting, Orville and Wilbur had become the first people in history to fly an airplane.

The *Wright Flyer 1* flew for the first time on December 17, 1903.

What Is Flight?

Insects, birds, and bats are the only creatures that can fly on their own. This means that they have enough power to lift themselves off the ground and move through the air under their own control.

A bat's wings are built to allow the bat to fly.

Birds flap their wings in a circular motion, which allows them to fly.

These creatures are built for flying. For example, when a bird flaps its wings, air moves faster over the tops of the wings than it does below them. That creates more **air pressure** below the bird's wings. Air pressure is the force that air puts on the things it surrounds. This air pressure pushes up on the bird's wings and makes flight possible.

How Do Airplanes Stay in the Air?

Unlike birds, people don't have the power to fly on their own. One way we can fly is in airplanes. They are the fastest form of **transportation** we have. Airplanes are big and heavy, so how can they fly?

Flight is made possible when the wings of an airplane push against air. The air pushes back. This action and **reaction** have enough force to allow the airplane to fly.

Most airplanes can fly from 500 to 600 miles per hour.

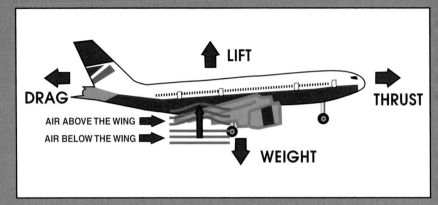

LIFT

DRAG

THRUST

AIR ABOVE THE WING

AIR BELOW THE WING

WEIGHT

What Is Lift?

Airplanes take off using an upward force called **lift**. Lift is caused by the difference in air pressure above and below an airplane's wings. Airplane wings have a special shape that makes lift possible. The top of the plane's wing is curved, and the bottom is flatter. Air passes over the top of the wing faster than under it. This makes the air pressure below the wing greater than the pressure above the wing, creating lift.

Lift works directly against the weight of the plane and allows it to fly.

How Does Lift Work?

This experiment shows how moving air allows a plane to fly.

- Cut a strip of paper about six inches long and two inches wide.

- Hold the shorter edge below your bottom lip. Let the paper hang over your fingers and chin.

- Blow across the top of the paper, and it will lift.

The slower-moving air beneath the paper lifts it up. This is how the slower-moving air under an airplane wing lifts an airplane.

How Do Thrust and Drag Work?

Thrust is the force that moves a plane forward. Thrust overcomes a force called **drag**. Drag is the force of air pushing against the plane as it moves forward. Thrust comes from **propellers** or jet engines. Propellers spin and pull planes through the air. Jet engines push out hot gases, causing the plane to move forward very fast when the pilot increases the engine power.

Thrust is the force that allows the pilot to change the speed of the plane.

How Do Airplanes Move in the Air?

When the pilot decreases the engine power, the amount of thrust is reduced, which slows the plane down.

A pilot uses **ailerons** (AY-luh-rons) to steer the plane and a **rudder** on the tail to help turn it. Flaps on the wings are lowered to help increase lift during takeoff. The flaps are also lowered to increase the drag when the plane is landing. These parts work together to allow the pilot to fly the plane.

Planes are built so that all the parts work together. This way, the plane can fly smoothly.

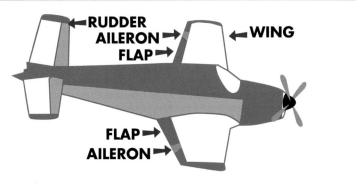

RUDDER
AILERON
FLAP
WING
FLAP
AILERON

19

All Kinds of Airplanes

Planes that do different jobs need special shapes or parts to do those jobs. Some planes have special gear so that they can land on water. Some are built to fly right into thunderstorms to study weather. Other planes, such as the crop duster, are used to spray crops so that bugs don't eat them. Crop dusters are also used to drop and plant seeds, such as rice and rye, over large areas.

This seaplane has special landing gear so that it can take off and land on the water.

The Fast Way to Travel

Since the Wright brothers made the first flight in 1903, airplanes have become bigger and faster. Large jets can carry more than 400 people at a time to places all over the world. Before there were airplanes, it would take days, weeks, or even months for people to travel to different states or countries. Today we can fly to different parts of the world in a few hours. Airplanes have made traveling easier and faster than ever.

Glossary

aileron   A part on the wing of an airplane used for turning.

air pressure   The force that air puts on the things it surrounds.

drag   The force of air pushing against a plane as it moves forward.

experiment   A test used to figure something out.

lift   An upward force caused by a difference in air pressure.

propeller   Spinning blades that pull an airplane through the air.

reaction   An action caused by a force.

rudder   A part on the tail of an airplane.

thrust   The force that moves an airplane forward.

transportation   The movement of people or goods.

Index